KU-521-426

Avalanches

Sandra Woodcock

Published in association with The Basic Skills Agency

Hodder & Stoughton

A MEMBER OF THE HODDER HEADLINE GROUP

Acknowledgements
Cover: Galen Rowell/Corbis

Photos: pp3, 25 Galen Rowell/Corbis; p6 Marc Garanger/Corbis; p12 Topham/Associated Press; p15 Nick Hawkes; Ecoscene/Corbis; p18 Associated Press AP; p20 Camera Press Ltd.

Every effort has been made to trace copyright holders of material reproduced in this book. Any rights not acknowledged will be acknowledged in subsequent printings if notice is given to the publisher.

Orders; please contact Bookpoint Ltd, 39 Milton Park, Abingdon, Oxon OX14 4TD. Telephone (44) 01235 400414, Fax: (44) 01235 400454. Lines are open from 9.00–6.00, Monday to Saturday, with a 24 hour message answering service. Emails address: orders@bookpoint.co.uk

British Library Cataloguing in Publication Data
A catalogue record for this title is available from the British Library

ISBN 0 340 80064 X

First published 2001
Impression number   10 9 8 7 6 5 4 3 2 1
Year   2007 2006 2005 2004 2003 2002 2001

Typeset by SX Composing DTP, Rayleigh, Essex
Printed in Great Britain for Hodder & Stoughton Educational, a division of Hodder Headline Plc, 338 Euston Road, London NW1 3BH by Redwood Books Ltd, Trowbridge, Wilts.

Contents

Introduction

Snow in the mountains is beautiful to see.
Every year more and more people go to
high mountains to see the snow.
Some go to ski or snowboard.
Some go to walk or climb.
But in the mountains, snow can kill.
Every year 200 people are killed in avalanches.

1   What is an Avalanche?

An avalanche starts when a large mass of snow
starts to slide down a slope.
Heavy snow on a slope moves very fast.
An avalanche can move
at 100 mph (160 km/h) – sometimes faster.
It is like a huge, moving wall of snow.

As it races down the mountain slope,
it can destroy anything in its path.
Trees can be snapped like matchsticks.
People can be buried in snow
or picked up and carried by the avalanche.
Houses can be smashed up.

Snow is beautiful but it can also be dangerous as this
avalanche shows.

Avalanches often happen
when there has been a fresh fall of snow.
New snow can be like fine powder.
It can be unstable.
Powder snow avalanches travel the fastest:
up to 150 mph (240 km/h).

Avalanches often happen
when there is a thaw.
Some of the snow layers start to melt.
The melted water below can cause
a huge slab of snow to slide on top.

When snow is unstable,
the smallest shock can start an avalanche.
The sound of church bells
can be the trigger.
Someone walking or skiing can be a trigger.

Every year more people want to
use the mountains for sport.
This means more people
will be victims of avalanches.

In areas where people live and work in ski resorts,
there are avalanche experts.
Their job is to make the mountains
as safe as possible.

The smallest shock can start an avalanche. Even the sound of church bells can be a trigger.

2   Avalanche Experts

Avalanches seem to happen out of the blue.
But experts who study avalanches
can sometimes predict them.
How can they do this?

They need to know all about the mountain.
They need to know about the layers of snow.
Each time it snows, a new layer is made.
Experts know how all the layers are different.
Some layers are hard and compact.
Some layers are soft.

The experts look for signs
that the layers are splitting.
In busy ski resorts
they go out every morning.
They test the layers.

Avalanche experts check the snow layers every day. They need to check how stable the snow is.

Eskimos have 100 different words for 'snow'.
This is because snow is always
in a state of change.
Experts study the science of snow.
They can understand tiny changes
that most people would never see.

Some experts work with computers.
They put details about the area into the computer.
They may use details of past avalanches.
They use maths to work out
where avalanches are most likely.

Computers can model
how an avalanche will move.
But how is all this data used
to make the mountains safe?

3   Avalanche Control

The experts cannot stop avalanches.
But sometimes they can control
when they will happen.
If a large area of snow is unstable,
a controlled avalanche can be started.
This is done by firing mortars (small bombs)
at the mountain slope.
This causes explosions and starts an avalanche.
In ski resorts, explosive charges can be laid
on the slopes.

Small avalanches can be started
when the ski runs are closed.
This will stop bigger avalanches forming.
In the Rocky Mountains in North America,
thousands of dollars are spent on explosives
to keep the ski slopes safe.

The teams that work on this
must have great fun.
One team gets to trigger
500–1000 avalanches every year.
The teams see it as a kind of war
against the mountains.

Sometimes it is safer to start a controlled avalanche with explosives.

Some roads are near to avalanche slopes.
An avalanche can block a road for weeks.
It is better to close the road
and start a controlled avalanche.
Experts make avalanches happen
when they want them to.
This means the risk to people is not so great.

Sometimes villages are at risk from avalanches.
Lives can be saved by slowing down an avalanche.
One way to do this is to plant trees
on the lower parts of the slope.

Snow fences built higher on the slope
can make the snow more stable.
Walls can be built to funnel an avalanche
away from the village.

But in spite of all this,
avalanches still kill people,
even in busy holiday areas.

Fences can help to make snow more stable. They can make an avalanche less likely.

4 Disaster in the Alps

The Alps are the highest mountains in Europe.
In the ski season, thousands of people
visit ski resorts in the Alps.
People have built chalets and hotels in safe areas.

The village of Montroc in France
was said to be safe.
In 1999 there had been no avalanche there
for 90 years.
But in February that year
there were heavy snow falls.

An avalanche crashed down
on the village of Montroc.
A huge wave of snow,
moving at 120 mph (190 km/hr),
ripped out rocks and trees.
Then the snow covered the village,
like a blanket of death.

Homes were buried.
Some people were lucky:
they got out in time.
But some were trapped under the snow.
People in the village had to look for their friends.
Rescue dogs were used.
They can be the best way to find people.
They can sniff out victims
faster than the machine sensors.

Rescue workers search for victims after an avalanche in the French Alps, 1999.

Under the blanket of snow,
some people were still alive.
Chalets had been turned upside down.
But under the broken walls and roofs
there were spaces free from snow.
People could breathe.
If they were found quickly, they could survive.

More than 20 people were rescued.
But 12 people had been killed
and 17 buildings were wiped out.
The road was covered with snow 10 metres
(30 feet) deep.

There were avalanches in other parts of the Alps.
People were killed skiing, climbing
and snowboarding.
Spring 1999 was a bad time for avalanches.

This avalanche crashed right inside a house in Sweden.

5   Inside an Avalanche

Some people have survived avalanches.
They can say what it feels like
to be carried down a mountain slope
at 100 mph (160 km/h).

The snow just picks you up
and throws you around.
Sometimes you can breathe
and sometimes you are choking on snow.
Your eyes, nose and throat are full of snow.
You are racing down a steep slope
with rocks and trees ahead of you.
But you can't control what is happening.
You go where the avalanche takes you.
The avalanche can dump you
a long way from where you started.
If you're lucky you will be found and rescued.
Perhaps you will have just a few cuts and bruises.

Many people don't survive.
Most die when they are slammed
against rocks or trees.
Some are choked by the snow.
Others die from extreme cold
before they are found.
Some people are lucky.

In 1998 seven people were climbing
in the mountains of Scotland.
An avalanche took them by surprise
and they were buried in snow.
Four of the group died.
But three people survived, trapped
under 1 metre (3 feet) of snow for 16 hours!
They were in a pocket of air.

6 Taking Risks and Taking Care

Mountain sports are risky.
There are always people who like to take risks.
They want to go outside the safe areas.
These are the people in most danger.

There are things they can do
which may save their lives.
They can pick the right time
to cross dangerous slopes.
Early morning is best,
before the sun has warmed the slope.

They can carry special gear
to help rescue teams to find them.
Some skiers trail a 10 metre (30 foot) cord
behind them as they ski.
If they are buried, some part of the cord
may be seen on top of the snow.

There are tiny micro chips
that can be fixed to clothes.
They give off a signal.
But the rescue team
must have a receiver to pick up the signal.

These walkers are trailing a long cord. It could help someone find them. An avalanche is already starting behind them.

Now there are special vests
which hold air under pressure.
In an avalanche the vest can be inflated.
This helps the person to float
on top of the snow slide.
A skier buried under snow
could even breathe the air from the vest!

Experts can do a lot
to make mountain sports safer.
Avalanche experts are learning more all the time.
But anyone who goes into an avalanche area
should know about the danger of a sudden white
death.